NECK OF A GIRAFFE

OF A

GIRAFFE

PEASANT TO PHYSICIAN

Josephine Okoronkwo, Ph.D.

NECK OF A GIRAFFE
PEASANT TO PHYSICIAN

iUniverse books may be ordered through booksellers or by contacting:

iUniverse
1663 Liberty Drive
Bloomington, IN 47403
www.iuniverse.com
844-349-9409

Because of the dynamic nature of the Internet, any web addresses or links contained in this book may have changed since publication and may no longer be valid. The views expressed in this work are solely those of the author and do not necessarily reflect the views of the publisher, and the publisher hereby disclaims any responsibility for them.

Any people depicted in stock imagery provided by Getty Images are models, and such images are being used for illustrative purposes only. Certain stock imagery © Getty Images.

ISBN: 978-1-6632-3976-1 (sc)
ISBN: 978-1-6632-3979-2 (e)

Print information available on the last page.

iUniverse rev. date: 07/06/2022

Dedication

To the memory of my dearly beloved parents, Reuben
and Annah Nwakaego Igwe Ezumah

Introduction

I faced obstacles as an undocumented immigrant widow raising five children in a faraway land with no family support. The last thing on my mind was writing a book on my journey of raising successful children. I never planned to write this book on raising successful children, especially raising two black male medical doctors, lawyer, DNP, Real Estate Entrepreneur, and Social Worker. Family and friends encouraged me to give the world my template. You must have a gene pool, a colleague once told me. A handful of family members and friends told me if I did not write it, they would write it for me." A colleague and dear friend, Mr. Joe Marion texted me: "Jo, you may want to put your family's educational achievements on TV's 60 Minutes. It is that remarkable. I will write em if you want me to". My family's educational achievement is not unique. I have African family friends with successful (children), doctors and lawyers. Be that as it may, let me tell my story before someone else tells my story. I decided to put pen to paper. Many ask me for a template. Some even go further to ask: "Dr. O, just give us the cheat sheet".

So, here is the book, a self-help guide of sorts, of falling down, picking yourself up and moving ahead. Stones maybe thrown at you; remain fearless, focused, and forge ahead. Use the stones as your building block, as your foundation. Beginning with becoming a "been to", and going through the story to living the glory. I hope I make sense to you. Nothing is left out. I share the journey with you, along with the potholes, detours and U-turns. Like an artiste once wrote, "nothing good comes easy". Many see the glory without knowing the story behind this glory. My journey started with a mindset, staying on that goal. Many people did not know what I was doing with my children. My six children, three boys and three girls, each had his or her unique aspirations. The boys loved football, played high school and college. My girls loved track and field and basketball. Of course education was the primary focus in my household. My journey began in Nigeria.

As you read the book, it is my hope that you glean something from it. You may cry, you may laugh, you may wonder, wow! and you would learn that it does not matter what obstacles and challenges come your way, you cannot allow your challenges consume you, you can overcome them. Be an overcomer. Tie your wrapper tight and strong. Time to flip the pages and read the story behind the glory. And, do not think that once you are in glory, your challenges are over. Life happens; challenge is still a part of life and it never ends until your expiration day, date and time.

Foreword

The book titled ***Neck of a Giraffe***, is written by a determined, focused professional- Dr. Josephine Okoronkwo-Onor. The title of her book is befitting of the symbolism of a giraffe, raising her neck to gaze and see far into the future, understanding what God has in store for her. Despite the devastating experience of losing her husband and father of her five children, (categorized by extreme shock and fear, in face of such a magnanimous adversity), Dr. Okoronkwo-Onor's focus allowed her to continue her life raising her children in a bubbling social environment, amidst a multitude of family friends with their families intact, - a psychology that can often have a ripple effect of a subdued and withdrawn personality.

Dr. Okoronkwo-Onor caught my attention in 1990 when I took a position at Dillard University in New Orleans, Louisiana, as an Assistant Professor of Political Science. Then, the President of the Association of Nigerians in New Orleans invited me to be the keynote speaker for the Nigerian Independence Celebration at the Holiday Inn. On that occasion, Nne Okoronkwo whom I call *"Ada Igbo"* was among the elegant Nigerian women who were displaying Nigerian Cultural dances and presentations. She continued to work at Southern University in New Orleans (SUNO) as Director of the International Students Program, while raising her children. In that capacity, she saw education from multiple prisms, and brought the impact to bear on her children at home. Her children continued to excel in sports, academics and eventually have grown to begin their own families. Josephine, you are to be commended for your faith and human energy, which you exuded in accepting your responsibilities, and accomplishing your goals and objectives. Another occasion that is worth noting is that while rearing her children, Dr. Okoronkwo-Onor became connected with her current husband, Dr. Onor, and they were blessed with who we today call, "Dr. Onor Jr." The smooth transition from a widow to a married woman again, all while pushing her children to work in a collective family enterprise, leads me to conclude that there is nothing God cannot do if you trust in Him.

Dr. Okoronkwo-Onor is a powerful woman of faith, strong will, with dynamic social ability. Dr. Onor was among the Nigerian women who showcased Nigerian Dances and Culture to Dr. Hassan Adamu, former Nigerian Ambassador to United States, during his visit with me at Dillard University. She featured prominently among the Nigerians and African World Network Organization Inc., the community that welcomed Dr. Adamu. She was among the Nigerian women who became surrogate mothers to my children, in the absence of their late mother, Mrs. Felicia Okorn. She distinctly acknowledged me in their work *ARISE* which showcased Nigerian Women's achievements in in the USA. When I left for Nigeria, Dr. Onor went ahead to pursue a Ph.D. in Public Policy, and now serves as an Adjunct Professor at Southern University, Baton Rouge, Louisiana.

Dr. Okoronkwo-Onor served in His Excellency, Prof. Charles Chukwuma Soludo's Transition Team of Anambra State. Okoronkwo-Onor, for your perseverance, your faith, your social agility, networking skills, managerial ability of your family, and your ability to survive under crisis, you are to be commended and congratulated. You have injected yourself into the community of objectivity and God will continue to guide you in all you do.

I am glad to write this forward for a dynamic and professional lady, Dr. Okoronkwo-Onor. Those who read her story will enjoy and grow. It is a must read.

PROFESSOR NCHOR BICHENE OKORN
BBA, MBA, MA, PH.D.
PROFESSOR EMERITUS OF POLITICAL SCIENCE
DILLARD UNIVERSITY
NEW ORLEANS LOUISIANA, USA

Acknowledgment

I simply acknowledge my family and friends, my friend and colleague, Mr. Joe Marion who called me up, wrote on my Facebook page that I must write my story before he writes it for me.

All my children who continue to love and care for me. All six of them: Emily, Gilbert, Irene, Linda, Michael and Gabriel. They too told me I must write my story because when they tell their friends my story, they think it is "fronting". My sincerest appreciation goes to all my children; they suggested vocabulary and provided guidance.

To my husband, Gabriel Onor Sr. who encouraged me immensely to put pen to paper. He was a great pillar. Thank you.

My parents, Reuben and Annah of blessed memory, who laid the foundation for the woman I have become, thank you. And to all my siblings for their love and support in all forms. I acknowledge my good friend, Dr. Nchor Okorn for writing the Foreword. My request to him was so informal and casual. And without hesitation, he replied, "I know you, just send me your CV, and the book and consider it done". And he did it glowingly.

And to all those shoulders too numerous to mention that I stand on and lean on, I thank you sincerely for all your support and encouragement. But I must mention my rock, my stronghold, my go to person, Dr. Chijioke Okoro, who was there for me and continues to be. Thank you.

1

TRAIN RIDE

I remember growing up with my siblings and parents in Kaduna, Nigeria. I was born there. I began my early education there until the 1966 Anti-Igbo Pogrom. This was not my first train ride from Kaduna to the East. During Christmas holidays, we often travelled home to my maternal grandmother's home. But this time around, this train ride was different. There was no holiday. So I wondered.

My mother took all of us and boarded a train headed for the Eastern part of Nigeria, specifically, Afikpo Road. In the second class coach was another woman with her children. We shared the coach room with her. I did not understand why we were leaving Kaduna. I was enjoying the train ride, looking at the landscape, enjoying the stops at various stations and mother buying us goodies. It was a two-day ride to Afikpo Road.

As the train approached a station close to a river, two young gentlemen knocked on our door and appealed to my mother and the other mother if they could hide beneath the chairs. They looked at the women with their wrappers on and advised them to use their wrappers to cover every opening beneath the chairs. They pledged to hold their breaths. My mother and the other mother obliged.

Twenty minutes later the train came to a stop on a bridge. There was a knock on the door. Four armed men walked in. They looked around and left, waved goodbye to us. What would have happened if those young men under the chairs were discovered? I wondered. We would all have been massacred? Or perhaps my mother and the other mother would have been arrested, jailed and killed? My mother and all the other mothers and women in that war were truly "underground" fighters, unsung heroines. Strong women. They saved lives.

When these unknown gun men left, and the train continued its journey crossing the bridge and headed East, the two men under the chairs emerged with tears rolling down their faces. They thanked the two mothers. They could not thank them enough. They were riding with the Train Guard in the guard's space with no space to hide. In their appreciation, they told my mother and the other mother they would have given them all their life's savings, but they jumped into the train with just the clothes on their backs as they cried and went back to join the Train's Guard. We continued our journey to Afikpo Road as they dropped off at Enugu. We arrived Afikpo Road late evening and boarded a bus headed to my maternal grandmother's village at Mbala, Isuochi. There was so much jubilation at that time of night of our arrival. The entire village woke up to receive us.

My dad waved goodbye as we boarded the train. This man taught me how to write, holding my fingers. He worked for the Railway station. We left him alone. At the heat of the "1966 Anti- Igbo Pogrom", he escaped and reunited with us.

Life of adjustment began for all of us. As a "township" youngster, I had to adjust to no electricity in the village. There was running water, but it was miles away, situated at the center of the town at the market square. Then, there was no running water in any home. I learnt what it meant to go fetch water from the streams miles away balancing the mud pot or bucket on my head. I also learnt how to hand wash clothes by the stream, dry them in the sun, fold them and place them in the basin around the bucket of water, balanced the basin on my head and walked back home.

2

MISS

They called me Miss. Female elementary school teachers were referred to as "Miss". Two of my aunties were called Miss. So, when I was called Miss, it dawned on me that I have grown up.

On completing my secondary school and passing my West African School Certificate, I did a stint with the Federal Radio of Nigeria at Enugu before I was posted to a small town called Ozara for a teaching job. I was there for one year before I was accepted to a Crash Teacher Training Program at Women Teachers College (WTC) at Old Umuahia. Umuahia is now the capital of Abia State.

One of my Teacher Aunties visited my older sister at Enugu on a holiday. I was visiting there too. She saw me and said: "Nne, what are you doing here? You should be at WTC". I said, how?

She said excitedly, "Your name is in the Daily Star, you have been posted to WTC", my auntie said. I was full of joy. Then, names of accepted students for Teacher Training Crash Programs were posted in major Nigerian Newspapers.

I packed my luggage and relocated to Old Umuahia. The Teacher Training Crash Program for one academic year was for only those who passed all papers in their West African School Certificate. I got there. My room was assigned to me. Classes began in earnest. There was structure. There was a time table for all activities including time to wake up, assembly time, breakfast and then classes. Because it was a crash program, students must pay serious attention to academics. I engaged in extra curricula activities like Debate Society and Drama Club. One play that I was part of was ***The Merchant of Venice*** by William Shakespeare. I played Portia. The community was invited to come to the Play. After playing Portia, I had serious suitors from the crowd, but I turned them down. I was focused on finishing the crash program strong.

Nne studying hard
at WTC, Umuahia

Upon my completion of the program, I chose to be assigned to Nzerem, a small farm settlement along Okigwe and Afikpo in Southeast Nigeria. Nzerem is one of many Aro Chukwu settlements in Southeast Nigeria. My paternal grandparents were among the first settlers. As the oral history goes, a strong and powerful woman named Nwamgbo founded this settlement and invited her immediate and extended family members to join her. Nzerem is rich in agricultural production such as yam and rice. My father grew up here before joining The Nigerian Railway Station. When my father retired, he moved back there. In less than three years of retiring to this settlement called Nzerem, his life was ended by a drunk driver.

I would come for holidays along with my siblings to spend some time with our parents. Nzerem became home. I fell in love with Nzerem. I participated in Debate Society with my peers. The villagers both literate and illiterate would gather in the school hall to watch us debate. In one of these debates, my step paternal grandmother nicknamed me "Mrs. Ekpo". She said, I argued like Mrs. Ekpo. This step paternal grandmother was the last of three wives of my paternal grandfather. My father's mother was the first wife. Mrs. Ekpo was a famous strong Igbo woman who organized a demonstration against taxation of Aba market women. This demonstration was popularly known as "Aba Women's Riot". Many who knew me then still call me Mrs. Ekpo.

The only school there, an elementary school became my passion. I dreamt of making a difference there. Upon completing my Crash Program at WTC, I became a teacher at Nzerem. I was called Miss. My mother was called "Mama Miss", and my father "Papa Miss". Many in the little town were shocked to see a young woman like me choosing to teach here when I had options to go teach anywhere.

I taught Elementary four. I poured my all into the young ones. My result was not out. So, my salary was just like a West African school certificate holder. Six months later, the result was out. I cleared my subjects. The next pay period, my headmaster, Mr. Eke rode his bicycle like he always did to the local government office to collect our salaries every pay period. I knew I would be paid my arrears. Mr. Eke was taking too long, I thought to myself.

One hour later, Mr. Eke summoned me to his office. I knew what it was about. He said, "Congratulations Miss, you cleared your papers and you were paid your six month arrears". All in cash. That was how we were paid. I ran home to my parents so elated. My parents were proud. My mother ran to the backyard, and caught the best live hen to slaughter to celebrate me. She made the best hen stew for dinner that day. The news spread like wild fire that Miss cleared all her papers, "she is intelligent", they said. My parents raised goats, sheep and hen. They were successful farmers with a huge barn of yam. We never had to buy yam, rice or fresh vegetables. The food was so organic. Suitors were coming for my hand in marriage. After a year, I got married and I transferred to the big city, Enugu, the then capital of the Southeast Nigeria.

Nne with her two children,
Udumaga and Onyekachi
Right is a village friend at Nzerem

In this little place, called Nzerem, it had smart men and women who cultivated the land and raised their children to be better than they are. Nzerem had many legends. One of them was a woman called Mama Chi. She had no children of hers, she was barren but she loved all the children and disciplined them. In addition to being a disciplinarian, she was a very well-known medical expert. She did not attend any school, whether elementary school or college. So medical school was out of the way. But she had traditional medical school training. She was known to be vast in every leave in the bush that would cure any ailment including eye problem. She was also a midwife. She delivered a lot of babies safely in the backyards of their families. Her fame reached all neighboring communities. She was an expert in "pediatrics". If a child had malaria, she would go to the bush, collect various leaves, boil them, and have the child receive steam treatment. The child usually got well after two or three treatments. I was once her patient. All the children respected and feared her. If a child heard that Mama Chi was coming to his or her sick bed, the said child would declare that he or she was well instead of receiving treatment from Mama Chi.

It was in this place that it dawned on me that many mothers consider their successful sons as "Ojukwu nwa Nnewi" On one of visits from the U.S.A., I went to pay a condolence visit to a mother who lost her successful adult first son. The first son was in my age group. As I entered the woman's living room, she started weeping saying "Ojukwu nwa Nnewi, a anwu" crying uncontrollably repeating the same line, meaning Ojukwu the child of Nnewi is dead. How can Ojukwu die, without an international Breaking

News announcement? How can I hear about Ojukwu's death in this little town? General Odumegwu Emeka Ojukwu was a defunct leader of Biafra, a highly regarded man in the Southeast. Unbeknownst to me, she considered her son as "Ojukwu nwa Nnewi" as did many mothers then and perhaps, now. The real Ojukwu did not die until after twenty-five years later.

This little settlement town of Aro Chukwu that I loved so much consisted mainly of mud houses with palm frond roofs. There were only a handful of cement plastered homes with zinc roofs. Those who were fortunate to live in such zinc roof houses were considered the elites. The town had four villages. Some of the villages had compounds of kit and kin. The biggest of these villages had the chief's house. The chief's door was always open. He had a huge front yard where the elders gathered for regular meetings and to settle land disputes and other delicate matrimonial matters among others.

I learnt how to swim in this place. There was a stream along the only main road that connects to other towns. This stream only filled up during raining season; during dry season it dries up. During rainy season every child looks up to fetching water from a nearby source instead of trekking three to four miles for water. At least, in this stream you can fetch water for household chores. But one still has to trek many miles for safe drinking water. The stream ran under a bridge. We would jump from the bridge into the stream. As a beginner in swimming, the "life guards" would push the beginners into the stream. Do not try this. We would scream for our dear lives; then they would jump in and teach us how to swim by "fire or by force". It was scary, but I learnt how to swim.

In this town, I learnt the importance of maintaining confidentiality. One Christmas, as always, there were many entertainments in the form of masquerades, singing and dancing to the beats of the drums, pursuing young women and men who dared them. It was always fun for a masquerade to pursue anyone. The runner could run into any front door. This particular Christmas before I became a Miss, I came home to celebrate Christmas with family and friends. After attending Church service and eating lunch with family. I got ready to go see the masquerades with girlfriends. The masquerades we ran into had a field day. They pursued us flogging some of us as we made our way into someone's front door. It was fun. We ran like we ran track as the masquerades ran faster than us. In this front door, I began to watch and observe other masquerades. One particular masquerade captured my attention. This masquerade walked and danced like one of my brothers. The drummers and singers were really good as the masquerade entertained the crowd with his expert dance moves. All cheered for him. This is my brother. I have three brothers and I have seen two of them not as masquerades, but as drummers and singers. This must be my brother, the masquerade. I came out of the front door and announced, that's my brother, the masquerade; I called him by his name. The masquerade charged, descending to flog me as I ran my fastest four hundred forty yards with the masquerade behind. Because I was his sister, he ran a little slower than I did, but was able to flog me as his drummers and singers burst into a song, "Nne tulata onu gi, tulata onu gi" meaning literally, "Nne watch your tongue" to the cheers of the crowd. This new song stuck within this town.

Miss celebratory Photo of clearing her Teacher Training Examination

3

BEEN TO

Leaving Nigeria for the United States of America was a dream come true. I completed my secondary and tertiary education in Nigeria. Got married and had two kids. My husband was a lecturer at the Institute of Management and Technology (IMT), a very smart young man. He received his undergraduate and graduate education (Masters level) on Federal Government scholarship and study leave with pay before he proceeded to the USA for a terminal degree again on a Federal Government of Nigeria's scholarship and study leave with pay. I was a teacher at an Elementary school in Enugu. I left teaching at the primary school and enrolled at Alvan Ikoku College of Education, Owerri. My husband left for the USA. I had one more year to complete at Alvan Ikoku College of Education. I wanted to travel with him. But Aunties advised me to the contrary. They said, "stay here and complete your education, in case you get there and do not go further. We have examples of wives who went with their husbands and came back empty handed. Life is hard there", they concluded. I listened. How could you not listen to your aunties? They are teachers, mentors and role models. I was raised to respect my elders, listen to them. I was getting ready to becoming "been to". You see, then, it was a special privilege for a young person to go abroad, United Kingdom and or United States of America and return to belong to that special class, "Been to".

One Christmas holiday when I was still in secondary school, one storied young man, called all the nearby youths together at Enugu to encourage us to stay in school, work hard, apply abroad and be like him. At the end of his presentation to us, he said, "breakfast in Lagos, lunch in London". All of us in that gathering wanted to grow up like him, "been to". "Been to" was the new badge of sophisticated elites.

At the conclusion of my final year at Alvan, I was looking forward to travelling to The U.S.A., a country I have studied in my elementary school days and secondary schools. Even at Alvan a handful of my lecturers shared their glowing stories in class. There is no "Free Lunch in America", they would tell us. "You must work hard", they would say. My husband returned and brought all of us, myself and two children- a girl- Emily Udumaga and a boy- Gilbert Onyekachi to the country with its streets paved in gold or so I believed. We arrived at a one-bedroom apartment in St. Louis, Missouri. All my expectations went with the wind. Why did I leave a life of luxury in a two-bedroom well-furnished flat to a one-bedroom scantly furnished apartment in "God's own country", I thought to myself? This cannot be the USA. I worried. He was a student. He would leave to go to classes, I stayed with the children. I often sat by the window looking out, counting all the cars that drove by, and all the pedestrians as they walked by. I was scared. Back home before travelling, I was warned by my mother and others to be careful, stay indoors because the country is violent. They shoot and kill. With this at the back of my mind, I was consumed with fear.

We had family friends, Igbo and Yoruba mainly who helped to calm my fears down. We lived in St. Louis from June to December of same year before relocating to Austin, Texas where my husband continued his doctoral education in Mathematics. By the way, he earned another master's degree in Systems Engineering at Washington University, St. Louis.

My husband had a very old Toyota corolla car. He serviced it for our trip to Austin, Texas. We packed up. The two children in the back of the car. He took the wheels. Driving for about eight hours, we decided to take a rest in a hotel. The next morning getting close to Oklahoma, the car broke down. A tow truck came and brought us to a mechanic workshop. They told us they would not be able to complete work on the same day. My husband, Emmanuel had to be in school the next day. We had to make a quick decision. Greyhound was the best bet. We took what we could and abandoned the car there with a few pieces of stuff we could not take. We arrived Austin. A Yoruba family we never met before was called to the International Office, and they picked us up. They had three children in a two-bedroom apartment. They did not mind housing us. A very kind and hospitable family.

I forgot an important box in the mechanic workshop in the trunk of the car. The box contained nick naps and inside one of the nick naps, I hid my only money-$500.00. I cried.

Emmanuel called the workshop and asked them to ship the box to us. I thought the money would be gone. I was wrong. Four days later, the box arrived, untampered with, and with my money intact. Thank you guys. This particular action helped build my trust in my new country-USA. My fears vanished.

Emmanuel enrolled in his doctoral classes, became a Teaching Assistant and the benefits that came with it, one of which was $50.00 tuition for a spouse. I took advantage of that and enrolled in same University-University of Texas at Austin. At Austin, I had my first American anchor child, a daughter, Irene Obianuju.

He completed his studies in record time, got a teaching at Illinois. We moved again. Again, after one academic year at that university, he got a teaching job with a University in New Orleans. Each university he went, I enrolled there. At this university, I completed my Bachelor of Arts degree in English graduating magna cum laude, free. Again, he got a teaching job at another University in New Orleans. In New Orleans, I had two more children, a girl –Linda Obinwanne and a boy –Michael Chikwendu. I followed him to this university for my Master's degree in Guidance and Counseling. In my second semester, darkness creeped in.

Emmanuel became sick, going back and forth the doctor's office.

4

DARKNESS FALLS IN DAYLIGHT

One terrible evening, Emmanuel came back from work feeling so sick. I took him to a hospital in New Orleans East where he spent four days before he was transferred to a Downtown New Orleans Hospital and finally to an Uptown hospital in New Orleans. We have already received the terrible diagnosis, cancer of the liver. He was in his last days the doctors told me. I was devastated and lost. What would I do with five children in a foreign land with no job and an undocumented immigrant? I was an undocumented immigrant. At the first university that offered him a job, they also sponsored him for the Permanent Residency or Green Card as it is famously known. We decided that he should file first and once he gets it, then Emily, Onyekachi and I can file. After he got it, he began to file ours not knowing that once he changed his status from a student visa (F-1) without including his dependent family (F-2), that we would automatically become "out of status" or undocumented immigrants.

Before he lost consciousness, he warned me in the presence of one of his sisters who came from out of town, his brother who just joined us from Nigeria, that I should not on any account accompany his body home. I must stay back with the children. This was an unacceptable proposition to my ancestral home. A wife must be present at the funeral of her husband, else she would be ostracized from the community. This weighed me down. My siblings in Nigeria warned me not to follow his death wish. This heavy burden weighed me down. What am I to do? Should I "carry my burdens with strength", as Egejuru (2011) writes. I was conditioned and saw how my mother and maternal grandmother carried themselves as very strong women. The sacrifices they made for us. I tied my wrapper tighter.

Emmanuel's first cousin, a medical doctor visited, had discussions with the treatment team. Emmanuel shared his death wish with him too. He spent a couple of days and left. He told me he would be in touch and he was. He was getting regular updates from the attending physicians. During the Nigeria Civil war, Biafra developed military ordinance called "Ogbunigwe", a deadly form of bomb that took many enemy lives. Young scientists were recruited to build this bomb in the laboratory. Emmanuel and other young men worked in the laboratory. Many surmise that many of the young men were exposed to the chemicals. Around the time Emmanuel died, a couple of these young men died too of same ailment. Research is needed to confirm this theory of exposure to the bomb making chemicals without protection to the young workers.

Josephine Okoronkwo, Ph.D.

I would wake up crying and praying all alone in the hospital room. I worried at night, one morning my undocumented immigrant status had a strong lead breaker. My first two children I had in Nigeria were also undocumented.

5

A LEAD LADY BREAKER

I was in the hospital room with Emmanuel lying on his sick bed. I was crying, praying and worrying, when I heard a knock on the door. I opened the door. A lady walked in. She looked at me and asked: "why are you crying, he is still breathing". I cried some more. She took me for a walk in the hospital, offered me coffee, coke and anything to see if I could calm down. I kept crying. She said, "tell me your issue". Growing up in Nigeria, I was taught not to disclose personal matters to external entities. It was a cultural code. Something inside told me to open up. You do not know from where cometh your help. I did. I shared my greatest issue- my inability to accompany the body home. She asked me why. I explained to her that I was an undocumented immigrant; I could go home but I would not be able to re-enter. She told me she did not understand; but would go back to the office to explain to her chairperson who would understand. The unfolding of solutions to our undocumented immigrant status began through this lead lady breaker. She walked me back to the hospital room with a promise- "this is the easy part of your problem". She was right.

The young lady was a colleague of Emmanuel in the Mathematics department of the university where he taught. An hour later after she left, a gentleman knocked on the door. He introduced himself. He reassured me that he would do his best to see that my immigration issue was resolved. He took the history of my case, in fact of our case. Remember my two older children we had in Nigeria were also undocumented. The gentleman said he would have a response to my case after playing Golf that night. In my mind, I pondered why after playing golf. What has golf got to do with my case?

The next day as he promised, he came back. He told me to go down to the Immigration office with a handful of documents and ask to speak with the Regional Director. I shed tears of relief; rushed home gathered all of our documents.

I was first in line in the Immigration office. I told them I had an appointment with the Regional Director. The customer service staff looked at me like, "are you sure"? I said yes. The customer service staff placed a call to the regional director to confirm. I was seated and had my one-minute interaction. He said, I am sorry about your husband's situation. but since he was still alive, you have to notify us as soon as he passed on. In addition, you must have a Financial Sponsor, someone who would attest that you would not become "a public charge". Who is going to be my Financial Sponsor? I thought to myself. Where else can I find one but to go to the university. I reported back to my point of contact at the university, the young man who played golf. He said, "do not worry, let me talk to the university President, a Priest. After two days, my affidavit of support was ready and signed by the President I never met, and would never meet. I picked up my Humanitarian letter and my travel was set.

6

I ACCOMPANIED THE BODY

At about 4:45 a.m., Emmanuel took his last breath. I cried and cried. The first person I called was his cousin, the medical doctor. He advised me to drive home carefully. I did. The news spread like wild fire. My community family rushed in, crying and consoling me, asking what they could do for me. My family in Nigeria was devastated, calling me non-stop. I was lost with five little children. I began packing our stuff to go home with the body and never looking back.

It was dusk. Where was his cousin, I wondered? I had a classmate and a good friend from Nigeria. She stayed with me consoling me until late at night when I received a call from Emmanuel's cousin from New Orleans airport to provide him with my address so he could catch a cab. My classmate and her husband volunteered to pick him up. He arrived and I felt relieved.

He cried and we cried. He looked around the house and asked me why were all the suitcases packed. He asked me why. I said, we were all going home and never coming back. "You must be out of your mind", he exclaimed.

The next morning, he accompanied me to the immigration office. The Regional Director was so compassionate, offered us coffee. After a few minutes, I was issued a Humanitarian Reinstatement of I-130 Petition letter with my passport photo attached to it. I was told to hold on to this letter with my life. The letter advised that I must re-enter within thirty days and after I return must begin processing our permanent residency. We left in amazement and thanking God. Is this possible? A university President sponsored our Humanitarian Reinstatement Petition.

The next challenge was finance. Then, there was no organized fund raising committee of friends to help raise funds for the bereaved. Today, there are fundraising committees for any death here or abroad where sometimes thousands of dollars are raised by families and friends. I was on my own. We just bought a house and a brand new car. His cousin and I went down to his university to see what benefits he had. He had a minimal benefit plan. Usually, the beneficiary could not collect any funds until all paperwork has been processed. His university loaned me money from his benefit plan for our trip. I must take my baby, Michael who was under two years old. Chinonyere and other family members insisted that someone must accompany me. A gentleman from my village who had his "papers" volunteered and travelled me. Papers, meant one who had his/her "Green Card" or citizenship. One of my aunties in the States came down. Akolam, Emmanuel's younger brother who just arrived on F-1 student visa became a great support for his nieces and nephews. So all three of us, myself, Mike and the young volunteer travelled home with the body.

Many family members and friends attended the cultural funeral rites. It was remarkable. My mother was my rock, though she worried how I would handle five children in a faraway land. She cried for her baby girl. A good friend of Emmanuel, a headmaster did not leave any stone unturned. Family and reliable friends were very supportive.

One early morning, many of the elders both men and women gathered in our house to bid me farewell to this far away land. After pleasantries were exchanged, the oldest man called the meeting to order. "Nne my daughter, what has happened, has happened. We thank you for completing all funeral rites. As you travel back to take care of your children, we call on God, our ancestors to guide you, protect and provide for you", he cleared his throat. The floor was now open. A younger woman took the floor, after the traditional greetings. "Mazi nile, nye Mazi, na umu ada, ndeewonu." She reminded all that Nne is a very young woman with five children and she has no resources. "So, let us not even inquire about their resources abroad", she took her seat.

A middle aged man, slightly built, a graduate of one of the universities in Nigeria who had a great job stood up, cleared his throat and was recognized and given the floor to speak. He was a "big man", in other words, a well to do person, married with children. His 504 Peugeot car that was freshly detailed was parked in the front yard. He was mixing English with the Igbo language in what we call "Engligbo". "Ladies and Gentlemen, umu nne m na umu nna m, we are gathered here early this morning ka anyi nye nwanne m anyi nwanyi, some "Ako bu Ije" meaning some guidance. Let me just say this upfront, the spirit does not talk, only a human being talks. When it gets to the point where you jump from one bed to another bed, make a U-turn and return home. You are too young, you can remarry. Mazi nile, orie ihe orie ihe, in our traditional greeting style, that's all I have for now". He took his seat. After all the wishes and prayers and libation, the early morning meeting came to an end. Of course, the small crowd was served special dishes.

7

RE-ENTRY

It was time to head back to the USA within the time limit specified on my Humanitarian document. Michael was really sick. We left my hometown, Aro Chukwu in Abia state. We had a layover in my auntie's place at Umuahia. Michael was still sick. We headed to Lagos to my sister's place. Michael was still sick. His temperature was being controlled with Tylenol, his diarrhea with Pepto-Bismol. I prayed to get back to the USA in a minute.

We left Lagos for New York via Nigeria Airways, a direct flight. Michael was still sick. We landed New York. He could not keep any food down in his stomach as I prayed to take us as fast as possible to the USA.

As we landed in the USA, New York, I presented our passports and the document signed by the District Regional Director of Immigration. Michael was born here. He had no issue of re-entry; I had. The immigration officer escorted us to the detention room. I pleaded that my child was sick, he had diarrhea. They gave me diapers. We missed our connecting flight to New Orleans. We spent hours in Detention before they finally cleared us. Perhaps, they thought I had fake documentation, or they were just doing their job.

We caught our late evening flight to the Big Easy, New Orleans. Michael was still sick. I could not wait for the next morning to take him to his pediatrician as walk in.

MALARIA PARASITE

My children's pediatrician's office was around the corner from where we live. I took Michael for doctor's visit. She prescribed medication. We came home, I gave the prescription to Akolam to go fill while I stayed with Michael. Michael's sickness took another turn as we were waiting for Akolam to come back from the Pharmacy. I rushed out of the house to my neighbor who immediately discerned the seriousness of Michael's state. He told me to enter his truck and he drove us like he was driving an Emergency Van.

The doctor took a look at Michael and jumped, abandoning all the other patients in her waiting room and drove us in her Mercedes Benz car to the nearest hospital. She called the emergency staff gave them instruction to prepare a bucket of ice as she sped on Interstate-10. At the emergency room, they put Michael in the bucket of ice with just his head sticking out. I was pacing back and forth crying. I was thinking another problem back to back? They drew his blood. A few minutes later, they told me he had many malaria parasites in his blood. When his temperature was controlled, he was transferred to a downtown Hospital. Michael asked me, "am I gonna die? How do I respond to this question? My dear, I told him, smile, God loves little old you like one of my Parish Priests says. I turned my back at him and shed tears, and asked God to have mercy on me. My flashback began. Why me? Why here?

After a week in quarantine at the hospital, Michael was discharged. Then in the hospital, he was quarantined like he had COVID-19 when COVID-19 first appeared. His room was sealed off. The residents, attending Physicians, nurses and all hospital staff came into the room in their Personal Protective Equipment (PPE). I was advised to stay out of the room, I declined, signed paperwork. I grew up in Nigeria where malaria was common, and I have never seen a malaria patient or his or her caregiver quarantined. Who would take care of my baby? How would I touch and feel my baby with cloves on, and the rest of the PPE on? I have suffered malaria in Nigeria. My mother nurtured me. I took care of Michael without PPE and never caught malaria.

IT IS NOT THIS EASY

I re-entered the country with a piece of document. I reported at the Immigration office as advised. I completed all necessary paperwork. I cannot afford an attorney to process our paper. The university had a Law school and a Legal Aid office. I ran to them. They told me that was the easy part that they could do for me. They did.

In a few weeks I received documents to take to a specific doctor for Udumaga, Onyekachi and for blood work. The doctor submitted our results to the Immigration office.

I received an interview date. I got my two children born outside the states ready, we set out for the interview. They had to miss school and they wondered why. Udumaga questioned why her other siblings were not going with us. I explained to her that they were born here. She was not satisfied. At the interview, I was nervous.

A young lady came out, greeted us and walked with us to the conference room. My heart was pounding. She verified our identities, gazed at me and said: "it is not this easy, congratulations she continued, you would receive your cards in two weeks". With God everything is easy. Tears rolled down my face as I said thank you, thank you. I was full of joy. I thank God, for His mercies endureth forever. I took a very heavy sigh of relief. God, is this how you work? He made it so easy. In less than three weeks, Udumaga, Onyekachi and myself received our Green Cards in the mail. One major problem is resolved within a year.

I travelled home for the one-year anniversary to complete all traditional funeral rites. Upon my return, I was touched by the generosity and denomination of my Financial Sponsor. I was born of another denomination. I grew up baptized in the denomination, sang in the choir and a Youth member. I could not help observing how caring and selfless my new found faith is. I reflected and evaluated how they were there for me, from the beginning to the end without asking for anything in return. Every help or service was Free, even when I wanted to present the President with an appreciation gift that I brought from Nigeria, he told his Assistant that he did not want it. As I write this, my eyes have not seen this President. He was kind, compassionate. All he knew and heard was my story and he took it from there. I changed my denomination, took my children with me. We got baptized. I will not depart from this denomination that picked me up when I was down and out. In my culture, they say that "okuko anaghi echefu onye turu ya nku na udu mmiri", meaning literally, one cannot forget someone who came to your rescue at your greatest point of need. I remain grateful and thankful to my new denomination.

10

THREE DOORS

Three wide doors opened as I was searching for a way out. Three families entered my life. The men of two of the families were Emmanuel's colleagues in one of the universities he taught. I am Igbo. One of the families was Yoruba, the other from Kenya and the last but not least, an Igbo woman. Nigeria is a country of many ethnic groups including Yoruba and Igbo. Often, they do not seem to get along. Sometimes, there is ethnic discrimination and misunderstanding. But, I have come to appreciate all knowing that "diversity is our strength".

A loving and caring Yoruba family, the Dewos, came to my rescue. A young couple with four children, they would pick up my kids each weekend, and dropped them off with so many goodies.

They initiated annual Christmas Carols. Mrs. Dewo would prepare assorted meals, lay out a basket full of various Christmas gifts. We would all gather a day or two before Christmas in their home with another family and their own children too.

The patriarch, Dewo had already prepared different Bible passages for each of the children and adults. There was a book of Christmas carol songs. We would sing, read our assigned passages, and then he would lead the discussion. At the end of the carol, the feast would begin. After the feast, the matriarch would invite all to pick and choose whatever gift he/or she wanted from the basket. I am indebted to this generous, caring and sharing God fearing family.

Throughout, they would stop by bearing food items, clothing and prayers. Our children became friends. Their footprints are embedded in us.

The Kenya family was fabulous too. Lo and his wife, Pat from The Caribbean were just too classy. Pat would wash, dry and iron her children's gently used clothes, along with grocery and ask her husband to deliver them to me. This was done frequently. One day, I was getting my hair done, and I received a phone call just one year into my relationship with this family that Pat just passed on. I screamed so hard and told my hair dresser to undo my hair. I must leave now, I said. My friend just passed on.

Ndaa was my confidant, my counselor, my mentor and my "older sister". Ndaa was an "acada" woman. In Nigeria in those good old days, women with university education were addressed as "acada" She affectionately called me, "Odogorofina", the way she said villagers pronounce "Josephine". This was really sweet to me. She provided professional and personal counseling to me though she was not a licensed counselor. But you see, where I come from, our elders provide the guidance that young adults needed to become productive citizens of the village and beyond. The elders were the teachers, the mothers and fathers, the counselors, the custodians of the culture. All of them together raise every child. The raising of children was not just the purview of the parents. In my Igbo culture, we say that, "a woman bears a baby, but the village raises the baby".

Ndaa and the others in this book, family and friends became my village in this place.

*   *   *   *   *

"If I stand tall, it is because, I stand on the shoulders of those who have gone before me and those among us", an African proverb says.

11

I TIED MY WRAPPER STRONG

Tough time rolled in. I still had to complete my master's degree. During Emmanuel's funeral in New Orleans, almost everyone present whispered almost same line to me: "Hang on, it is going to be okay, it is well". One person's whisper was different. He whispered to me: "Josephine get your education, do not quit or stop. Education is your key to the future". I looked at him and nodded. It stuck with me.

With no job, my mortgage, car note, utility bills and many mouths to feed, I often stayed inside crying and crying as the children were in school. One day, a call came. The caller said: "we are pleased to offer you a Teaching Laboratory Assistant's position in the English department beginning in August". I responded, I did not apply for any job. The caller continued, "I know, we chose you because you were our top graduating student". I speak the English language with an accent, but I do not write it with an accent. In my Alvan Ikoku English Education preparation, I took a course in English Phonetics. We had a Phonetics

Laboratory. The Lecturer taught us how to accurately pronounce English words. We practiced and practiced, yet, I still speak the language with an accent, though reduced accent. We had head phones. Our reading passages were recorded and played back to us. I went from this fulltime job, to a weekend Advisor in another university and to another a university where I worked for three decades and a few years. After all these decades, and retired, I moved on to a second career. I was offered a Public Board Trust position with a Federal Agency of the USA. In my autumn years to reach this second career move is truly an American Dream come true. My dream in elementary school, all I read about America, I am experiencing it. Only in America, as they say. A girl born in Kaduna, lived in all these villages with humble beginnings can truly confirm that education is an "equalizer" and "a key to one's destiny. That the USA is "a land of opportunity" if one works hard and smart. As you work hard and smart, stay away from illegal activities that would mess up your background check for your career whether in public or private service. One thing is clear in the USA, it is a legally structured society where one's record follows the person. As an immigrant, a paper citizen or even a born USA citizen, it is important to keep your records stainless. No one can deny a person's destiny, destiny can only be delayed, it is said.

In my part time position in a university, I would pack my lunch. One day, as I was eating my lunch, someone entered my office. He was a professor. He told me that he was following the food, it smelt so good, he said. I gave him a spoon to taste the food. It was goat meat jollof rice. I offered him only a taste, but he finished it. "Can I pay you to fix this dish weekly for me, he asked. I smiled. He was serious. A side business opened up for me. This same professor suggested that I share my cuisine with New Orleans.

Jazz Fest and other festivals around town opened up for me. The New Orleans Jazz & Heritage Festival, popularly known as "Jazz Fest" is an annual music, art and culture of New Orleans heritage that is a global attraction. I quickly applied, presented my proposed food items to the select tasters and was immediately selected for the upcoming year. That year's Fest was already over. Then, the First African Restaurant and Market emerged. Customers came from all over. I hosted some well-known Nigerian Musicians like Oriental Brothers and Oliver De Coco. These artistes drew a huge African crowd. My customers were diverse. They came from the Greater New Orleans. I cooked homemade meals for my customers. A handful of my African customers ordered weekly meals of egusi, ogbolo, stew and jollof rice from. I prepared "weekly "Happy Hour" meals for the only popular African Night club. During Black History Months, a handful of schools contracted me to serve African dishes.

I tried my hands in every legal business idea. My professional career was just beginning and my food business was booming. I had three jobs to pay for my mortgage, car note and all the other stuff I was not used to. I was raised in a culture where once you own a house, it is paid for. Anyway, this is for another discussion.

I was cooking in Jazz Fest: goat meat stew, akara, fried plantain and chin chin. Chin chin opened the door for my enterprise. I would balance a tray of fifty bags of chin chin on my head and walked among the crowd. The crowd plucked them off my head and paid with good tips. I worked so hard, relied on the skills and strength I acquired growing up. I was cooking at all the Festivals in New Orleans, Black History Fest, Caribbean Fest.

I met challenges, obstacles and opportunities. I had to evaluate my strength. I was overlooked, talked about. But in all these, I stayed fearless and focused with my number one priority: educational excellence for my children as I anchored my hope in God. I tied my wrapper tight and strong. A woman must tie her wrapper tight and strong so that it does not slip off your waist. You must not let your guard down. Strong women must tie their wrappers tight and strong to survive whatever comes her way. We must survive.

Josephine(Nne) selling chin chin at her first
Jazz Festival in New Orleans, 1989.

12

DON'T FORGET ANY

Then in my journey, I had five lovely children: Udumaga, Onyekachi, Obianuju, Obinwanne and Chikwendu. Their pediatrician often joked with me whenever I brought them for their vaccinations and or treatment for cold and what have you. Their Pediatrician was not far from our home. A lovely and caring pedestrian whose Office manager was her mother. After the doctor's visit, the doctor would remind me, "don't forget any".

A handful of people wondered what would become of these children. My mother would call me from Nigeria crying and asking me how we were doing. My siblings did too. My mother often told me to "tie my wrapper very strong, don't give up. Pray and pray". Pray and pray we did together. The sudden death of my father did not "kill" my mother. But the death of her adult baby son "killed" her. "Nothing hurts badly like the death of a child", my mother would say. My mother became a wreck. And, she never survived the death of her baby boy. She died shortly after his death.

My children and I bent our knees to Him above. My sister's friend in Lagos gave me a daily prayer book. Each evening, I gathered my children, we read the daily passage for that day, sang Igbo gospel songs which I taught them. We stayed together, sharing and caring. Managing whatever we had.

One particular Igbo gospel song that gave me strength and still gives me strength is the following song:

"Kwere, O ga-adiri gi mma, e kwere na aha Jesus,
O ga-adiri gi mma".
"Believe, it shall be well with you, if you believe in the Name of Jesus
It shall be well with you".

This song became our gospel mantra song. My children still sing it in their lives today.

I was like a giraffe, sleeping for only a few hours each night. I had these jobs and my restaurant business. I would stay up to prep food for the next day. I would kill goats. Killing goats in my culture is reserved for men. It was unheard of for a woman to kill a goat. I killed goats. Women are not supposed to kill goats in my part of Nigeria. I am here where I could engage in any legal activity without gender discrimination. I always took my young son, Onyekachi with me in case my cultural background hits me. I could defend myself and say, after all, there was a male with me.

Udumaga, my first born became a second mother to her siblings when I was working. Sometimes, she helped in the restaurant and at the festivals. The other four were too young to do anything. Udumaga and Onyekachi witnessed the struggles their mother went through.

Onyekachi is my oldest son. I would take him with me to various locations in the Greater New Orleans area to buy live goats, kill them and bring them home to cut up. He would assist me in every way I directed him. He watched his mother kill goats reserved for men in my place.

There were ups and downs. Lights, water, telephones would be in danger of disconnection. One time, our house was placed in foreclosure. Chinonyere came to the rescue. There were rumors that "Nne's children are not doing well". I ignored those rumors and continued to hustle and stayed on the priority.

I never forgot any of them whether at the doctor's office or anywhere else for that matter.

13

MGBORO OCHA

"Nne" as I am known among family members and close friends was born in Kaduna, in the northern part of Nigeria. As a child, I remember relocating to the eastern part of Nigeria as the Anti Igbo Pogrom was beginning. Nne lived with her blind maternal grandmother at Mbala, Isuochi where I completed my First School Leaving Certificate with distinction. Indulge me to share some of my early experiences that helped shape and kept me focused on my number one priority: educational excellence.

My grandmother, fondly called Mgboro ocha by her peers. Mgboro was her birth name. Because she was considered light skinned by any standard, "Ocha" meaning, light, was suffixed to her name. She was tall and a village beauty. I was named after her. She fondly called me "Ogbom", meaning namesake. Mgoro Ocha's eyesight failed later in life; she was not born blind.

She was the second wife of my maternal grandfather. She had four beautiful daughters. My mother was the first. My mother had elementary education. The second and third daughters grew up to become teachers. The last had some secondary education and became a tax specialist in the state's Tax office.

My grandfather's first wife had two sons. The first son eventually rose in his legal profession to become a Judge and the second son also rose in his career to become an Ambassador. Both were "London trained", meaning they received their university education in London. My grandfather's third and final wife had no children. We were told that she was barren. She would wake up early in the morning, leave the compound and would come back late at night. When everybody was sleeping, you could still hear her pounding her mortar. She was nicknamed, "o jee ije bee anyi", meaning "Journey walker". She made the best coconut rice which she shared with some of us her favorites. I was one of them.

Growing up with uncles and aunties and others who are highly educated, they became my role models and guided my mindset on education as "an equalizer", and molded my interests and values thereof.

Each wife had her own house in the compound. My grandfather struggled to raise his family and specifically to send his sons to acquire western education. Then, male children had preference in benefits and inheritance rights. My grandfather was a trader of palm kernel of sorts. He lived in Igbagwa, a small town near Nsukka in Enugu state. Often, he told me that many people avoided him and considered him foolish to overlook himself for the sake of his boys and girls. Look at it now, he chimed, I am laughing last and best. Nne my grandchild, whenever you grow up, get married, have children, invest in your children, they are your anchor in old age".

Mgboro ocha did not allow her disability keep her dependent. She became blind later in life. She accepted the fact that she must rely on another person's eyes. She had mental notes of where rooms, items were in the house. Her children built her a nice small disable accessible home. She could cook. She cooked the best food I have ever had. Before, I left for school, she would make sure I ate. As I came back, snack, food was ready for me. Then she would tell me to go study. "I want you to be number one in your class, look at your aunties and uncles", she would say. And, I read *Things Fall Apart*, *No Longer at Ease* by Chinua Achebe, *The Man Died* by Wole Soyinka and *Efuru* by Florence Nwapa and some other authors in Elementary six, books my uncles and aunties read and left in the bookshelf.

I was my grandmother's sight dog. I walked her to Church, village meetings, funerals, naming ceremonies and what have you. I stayed with her. In the evenings, every child participated in evening prayers. It was not mandatory, but every child understood that he or she must attend the prayer meeting. For the evening prayers, a Dede would ring the bell around the village chanting: nwoke bia, nwanyi bia, ekpere, come male, come female for prayer. Parents would send their children to join. Dede would then lead us to the village square "nkoro, ogbete". We would sing choruses, and then took turns in praying in Igbo.

After the evening prayer, I joined other children under an orange tree for moonlight stories, music, dance, proverbs and games. We were taught how to introduce a story and how to end it. Oral tradition was popular. We were taught life lessons through these stories. What happens to a liar, a thief, a disobedient child and so on and so forth. Most of the stories revolved around animals, lion, elephant, giraffe and especially the tortoise. On weekends, I became a letter writer and reader for many of the adults in the village. Many of the villagers were illiterate, but they had educated children with white collar careers in the big cities. Then there were no telephones. The only means of communication was through letters. I kept their family issues confidential. The children worried about their parents' health, inquired whether they had received the parcels they sent through a local courier. Parents would tell me to ask their children, how they were doing with their lives. I was in the Choir and Youth too. In the choir, I excelled as a tenor.

Living with my grandmother prepared me for womanhood, life issues and keeping my eyes on educational excellence. I graduated top of the class for my First Leaving Certificate and I was celebrated. My grandmother was so proud. I felt bad leaving her for secondary school.

MY ROOT

I cannot forget where I come from, who I am, how I got here and where I am headed. I am grounded in my root. I was blessed to have been surrounded by uncles and aunties, siblings and other distant relatives with education, knowledge and what I considered "Living their Best Lives". They lived in special gated communities, nice homes both in the cities and in the villages. I did not want life any other way, God willing. Many of their children were in universities. This consciousness stayed in me. There were a handful of widows who tied their wrappers tight and continued raising their children. One strong woman comes to mind. Akunnaya (Aku).

That's my foundation. I went back to what I knew, and took what was good.

Akunnaya or Aku as she was called lost her husband at a very young age. A village beauty and a school teacher, she continued her teaching and juggled it with petty trading. Her late husband was a renowned business man who traded in cement. He died in a motor accident. They had two sons and a daughter. Their daughter was the youngest.

Aku cried. The umuada made her go through the full and complete traditional funeral rites. The umuada are the first daughters of the extended family, comprising both old and young women. They are to be respected, adored and feared. No married woman that I know of wanted to have any interaction with umuada. They shaved Aku's head following the death of her husband. Early mornings, they made her wail and cry for two market days (two weeks). In the wailing and crying, Aku would sing praises of her late husband. She had to wear black for one full year. They monitored her movements and behavior. If they felt she was getting out of line, they called her to order. Aku could not wait for one year to be over. She confided in one of her aunties that they made her feel she killed her husband. "I was not in the car; she would say". Her Auntie, Uche told her the gossip. "You have not heard? The gossip is that you used juju to kill him early so that you can take his wealth". Unfortunately, it is often the belief in my part of the world, that no one dies of natural causes. Someone else killed the dead using voodoo/juju. "But you did not know that your husband's brothers would come for his wealth", she concluded. Sure enough, her brother –in-laws inherited all the wealth notwithstanding that she had two sons and a daughter. Aunty Uche confidentially counseled her niece to plan to transfer out of town or even state after the mourning period.

After one year, Aku picked up the pieces, her three children and relocated. Life was not easy for Aku and her children, but she preserved. After twenty years being out of town, she visited home with her children during Christmas season, now grown, the two sons became physicians and the girl a lawyer. This was Aku's season. The children began to build a mansion and the boys began to search for their wives. But mom had set standards. "Your prospective wives must be university graduates or "acada women" as university female graduates were known as when I was growing up.

But the first son, Emeka, fell in love with a village beauty with just a high school education. Mama objected to Emeka's choice. Mama insisted that the young woman, Chioma must enroll in a university and that is the only way that she could give her approval and blessings. Emeka told Chioma. Chioma was unhappy. She said, "why would you listen to your mother?" Emeka responded, "my mama raised me and always wants the best for me. If you love me, enroll in a university. It is for our own good. Mama has standards", he concluded. Chioma accepted and the rest is history.

The second son, Chidi, took good notes. He found himself a fellow physician and they got married. Adanna, the only daughter of Aku was swept off her feet by a rising politician with influence and power. Aku thanked her God for not putting her to shame as she began the next phase of her life-omugwo. Omugwo is when a mother spends at least one month in the home of any of her children who has just given birth to a bouncing baby, takes care of mother and child, leaves with gifts and goes to the next stop.

Josephine Okoronkwo, in the doorway of her restaurant.
Photographer: Thom Scott, taken 04/27/1991 and
published in The Times Picayune, May 07, 1991

15

A DIFFERENT WINE CARRYING

My root has many traditional activities I cherish. The New Yam Festival, Naming ceremony among others. One traditional event that I cherish the most is the wine carrying. My ethnic group prides themselves with Igba nkwu nwanyi meaning wine carrying for the traditional Igbo marriage. This was the Igbos only form of marriage before the coming of the West. Before the West met the South, Igbos did not have the "white wedding", we only had the traditional wine carrying. There are at least three stages that must be completed before the wine carrying. One critical stage is the "background check". Both the groom and bride's family begin to check each family out. Things like checking out each family's reputation, respectability, credibility, health status, credit check, etc. When all these elements are cleared satisfactorily, then the wine carrying is scheduled. The wine carrying signifies that the bride and groom's families have all agreed, set a date for this huge village celebration. No invitation is needed. All in the village and beyond is invited.

It is a joyous and colorful occasion. Young women look forward to their wine carrying day.

Kolanut or "oji" is a central item in this occasion. In Igboland Kolanut is a major celebratory item that must be presented to all to welcome all and to call on God and our ancestors to surround us with love, guidance and protection. It represents a symbol of welcome. If one fails to present Kolanut at an occasion, it can be monetized. The presentation of Kolanut requires special skills and knowledge of who to present it to first and how to present it. There can be commotion if presented to the wrong person first. "Oji na-eje ije" meaning literally that Kolanut walks. Kolanut must get to all titled men. Kolanut is reserved for men only to present, women partake in the eating only.

A different kind of wine carrying I witnessed while growing up exist in Igboland. In Igboland while I was growing up, I observed that male children are given special privileges and accorded much regard than female children. My father told us of how he was despised when my mother had a third baby and it was a female child. When family and friends asked him what his wife had this time, he told them. And their response was, "another baby girl, and you are proud to announce it". The fourth child is a male, the first male, and the sixth and seventh are males.

When a married woman fails from no fault of hers to have a male child, she feels disrespected and disregarded. She feels that she is cursed with no heir. So this woman is left with one option, perform a different kind of wine carrying. Her family and friends would encourage her to do this and they engage in searching for a suitable female who could come in and bear her a son or sons. This type of wine carrying is not elaborate and colorful as the one between a man and a woman. This one is woman to woman without any kind of sexual relationship. The older married woman who could not bear a son or sons "marries" a woman. All the stages of traditional marriage processes are done except that the sperm donor must be selected. The elderly states men search for a young man who is physically fit, unmarried yet. At dusk, the elderly statesmen and the sperm donor gather at the woman's house who just "married" another woman. The elderly states men perform the traditional rites including libation and informing the sperm donor that the young woman is his to impregnate her. The couple exchange sips of palm wine to the cheers of the statesmen and the woman husband. They eat and drink and disperse. This is usually done quietly and secretly so that the entire community does not know about the sperm donor. When a child from such relationship is born, many begin to guess his or her father from the resemblance. If the first child is a male, the woman husband feels fulfilled and organizes a huge naming ceremony.

16

AIRPORT MATCH

On the day of my return visit to the USA. I went to the International Airport in the day time, to check on my status, if my name was in the manifest. I walked into the airport and settled into the airlines' office. There was a short line. Then, one must check in with airlines early to ensure that your name is in the manifest to fly out. Against a beautifully air-conditioned and an executive backdrop office, the clerk at the counter asked for my Passport and Ticket. I handed her my documents. "Aunty, your name is in the manifest, make sure you check in at least two hours before departure time", the clerk said. I responded, thank you.

As I was walking to exist the airport, two gentlemen were gazing at me like they knew me. I stared back at them and recognized one of them. We greeted. One of them asked: are you visiting home? I said yes. Both of us live in New Orleans. We did not know each other personally. He was one of my customers in my small business.

As he would later inform me, the other gentleman with him inquired about me. He told him, that I just lost my husband and I had two kids or so. The man said to him in our language:" ihe I na-acho na uko elu di na uko ala". It simply means, losing its translation a little bit: "What you are looking for in the attic, is in the kitchen".

I had no idea that this man taught in the same university where I got my first professional job. One morning as I was walking to my office on my new job, a yellow Volvo car cut in front of me and the driver said, "Good morning, and what are you doing here", I responded, going to my office.

That man was Gabriel. He courted me. And so, I remarried. Another challenge faced me. I drove him to a hospital in the Greater New Orleans for a scheduled surgery. The Nurses prepared him for surgery. They gave him Penicillin by intravenous IV and left the room. Before all these, Gabriel and I were having normal conversation until about ten minutes into the intravenous IV, he began to slip to the other side. He stopped engaging and losing consciousness. I am not in the medical profession, but I knew something was not right. I ran out of the room, screaming "Doctor, Doctor". One doctor ran after me and inquired what was amiss. I only yelled Room 303 as I ran to that direction with the doctor running too. As soon as the doctor ran into the room, he pulled off the intravenous IV. Within two minutes, Gabriel began to regain his consciousness until he came back fully. I write this to say that I was terrified, my mind was messed up of thinking about another husband dying. The world may think that I am a "femme fatale". That was twenty-eight years ago.

We have one child together, Gabriel Ikechukwu Onor Jr. Gabriel is a very smart man, a Lion. A lion because he received his undergraduate degree from an "Ivy League" university in Nigeria whose mascot is a lion. I was told that in his hometown Nise while he was growing up, if someone counted about five young intelligent people, without counting him in, then the person doing the counting must be an enemy. That's how smart he is. Little wonder that even after a terminal degree and teaching in a university, he did not stop. As he told me, his passion is Medicine. He was haunted by his dying father's pronouncements. He told me that then in his home town there was only one physician from one part of the town, and his father told him that "he must be the doctor from the other part of the town" as his father took his last breadth. In our first year of relationship, he followed his passion. And it came to pass, that he became that doctor from the other part of the town. Many doctors have emerged in his hometown today including Ike, our son.

When Ike was five years old, we visited Anambra state. We landed at Abuja, stayed with my younger brother and his family. On our second day, we visited my oldest brother and his family at Bida in Niger state. We chartered a Coaster that took us to Bida. We made arrangements with the Coaster driver and his conductor to come the following day by my brother's residence to take us to Onitsha to visit my husband's younger brother and other family members. The driver was excited. He dropped us off by my brother, waved us goodbye, and we said we shall see them in the morning.

My younger brother welcomed us back. We informed him of our travel arrangement with the driver. He stared at us and said, "are you serious, you are making it too easy for the driver and co to plan evil against you, Americana, he concluded. He told us he will dismiss them once they arrive. First thing in the morning, the driver and his conductor arrived, blew the Coaster's horn. My brother came to the balcony of his two story house and asked them if he could help them. They responded that they are here to drive us to Onitsha. My brother convincingly and gently informed them that one of our cousins picked us up early this morning for Onitsha. They looked bewildered. Meanwhile Gabriel and I were looking at them through the window.

My brother informed us that we should never make transportation arrangement or any arrangement for that matter with unknown people, we make ourselves easy prey. He made arrangements for us and we got to Onitsha safely.

We went to Nise, his hometown. Gabriel would make frequent stops whenever he ran into relatives and friends. They would just gaze at me as if I was from Mars. On two occasions, in separate incidents, two gentlemen ordered me to get out of the car to assess me. I was reluctant, but they were serious. I got out. As if in unisom, each of them said, "you are okay, Nna, ebe ka isi fuo onye? meaning where did you see her.

Ike fell in love with Nise, Onitsha and Lagos. He was fascinated with Pure water. Pure water is water that is packaged in plastic sachets chilled in many cases, and hawked along the streets of major cities in Nigeria. He met many of his cousins and extended family members. At Onitsha, he would participate with other children in regular prayer meeting in the ground floor of his Uncle's house where we stayed. I was watching him from the second floor of the house. Ike's first cousin always brought him to the prayer meeting. On this day, his cousin introduced Ike to her young friend. The young friend culturally "hit" him and said "welcome". Ike began to really punch her. Ike's cousin tried to restrain Ike. I ran down the staircase to see what was amiss. Ike told me that girl "hit" him. I said, Ike, you are wrong. I explained to Ike that that is a method of excitement of welcoming people who just arrived. Ike misunderstood the young girl's welcome excitement as been violent. This was a teachable moment of cultural misunderstanding. Ike apologized.

I began to understand that God does not make mistakes.

17

EVERYBODY IS SOMEBODY

The neck of a giraffe aptly describes all the accomplishments of all my children, six of them and myself. I have a mixed bag of children who run the gamut, some took the straight trajectory from early life to the pinnacle of their dream careers. Others took a circuitous route and reached their dream careers. My people say, "the destination of a runner, is the same as the destination of a pedestrian or walker". One's destiny can be delayed but cannot be denied. Each of my children turned obstacles into opportunities. One by one they excelled to the amazement of many. Their accomplishments are truly longer than the neck of a giraffe.

I had a consciousness, a foundation I fell back on. I faced obstacles. The obstacles became my springboard to forge ahead, overcome them and achieve success. The families, friends I met during my dark days supported me in one way or the other, in spite of the fact that I was overlooked by many. Everybody is somebody, do not overlook anyone because a nobody today may become somebody tomorrow in the presence of everybody. God prepares tables in the presence of one's enemies. Stones were thrown at me. I remember my mother used to call me frequently in her crying voice, saying, "Nne, stones will be thrown at you, use those stones to build your foundation. Tie your wrapper strong. Whatever people say about you, let them say", as she hung up the phone. In this place, USA, I have heard this line: "Haters add flavor to your favor". I continued my journey, though with its rough and tumble, surviving the stones and with haters adding flavor to my favor, and now with this book, <u>Neck of a Giraffe</u>.

18

STRAIGHT AND CIRCUITOUS PATHWAYS

Each of my children is unique with his or her mannerism. I love all of them equally. Growing up in Nigeria, I saw how showing favoritism to a child who makes the most money breeds fracas in a family. My mother often told me, to love all my children equally, whether one has it and the other does not. She told me many stories dressed up with idioms on raising children. "You must love all your children equally, but do not spoil any", she emphasized.

One story was about eating from the ground literally and climbing your way up the table. Raise your children instead of raising your house helps. Let your children do the house chores, clean, cook, wash, dry and iron. I never had house help in the USA, could not afford that luxury. She would cite examples of families who raised their house helps, and the huge positive outcome for these house helps; whereas the children turned out to become "the useless children of so and so". "Have structure and be strict with your children, do not become their friends, pray with them", she would tell me. I incorporated these in raising my children.

Some of my children had a straight shoot to their professions and others made a detour, a-U-turn and circuitous pathways to their professions. After a detour, a, U-turn, getting to one's destination is the key. It is said that "one's destiny can be delayed but not denied". So never let your destiny be denied. Yes, there could be detours, U-turns, potholes, keep driving till you get to your destination.

I AM THE OLDEST

Emily Udumaga, my first child was born in Nigeria. Her middle name which is Igbo means "my fame spreads". She was a toddler when we left Nigeria. She lived with my mother, her grandmother when I was finishing up my tertiary education at Owerri and her dad was already in the United States of America. She picked up some Igbo language. As a child, she has always been assertive, argumentative and often wins the argument. We nicknamed her, Lawyer, Ikpeama". Lawyer Ikpeama was a very well-known lawyer in Nigeria, who won almost all his cases. Ikpeama meaning, one who never loses a case.

Many people call her my twin. We look alike and she has many of my mannerism. In Elementary school, she flourished. She would always write a complaint about issues at school, such as cafeteria food, uniform matters and school environment. A people person, she loves to treat everyone equally without regard to their background. Many call her Emily; I call her Udumaga. Udumaga became a second mother to her siblings. She took care of them whenever I was out hustling. She cooked too.

In high school, she excelled. She had a job too, brought in income to help her mother. She worked in a fried chicken kitchen brought home fried chicken along with fries. Her scores in Standardized Examinations such as SAT and ACT earned her a full scholarship (housing included) to study Pharmacy at The University of Houston. I was so excited and thankful to God. She accepted this offer among others. How would she get there? Houston is only about six hours drive from New Orleans. But I had no reliable car to take her there. I called on my go to person, Okenna who has relocated to Houston.

I narrated my ordeal to him. He said, "Put her in Greyhound bus, give me her arrival time and leave the rest to me". I wiped of my tears. I got off the phone and shared with Udumaga how she would get to Houston and how Uncle Okenna would pick her up and drop her at the campus. Understanding her mother's situation, she was grateful.

We went off shopping for every little thing she would need in college. Bedsheets, blankets, towels, bath soap, snacks. We packed up two suit cases. She knew Uncle Okenna already, so she would recognize him at the Bus Terminal. I booked her Greyhound Ticket. Okenna was informed of her arrival time. My extended family in Houston supported her during the course of her studies.

"It is not about sending your child to college, she needs a car too" one or two people told me. My response was: Thank God for Public Transportation. She lives in the dorm. "It is not about how you started, but how you end up." I remembered my mother's admonishment: "manage with whatever you have". I have raised my children through management.

I dropped Udumaga at the Bus Terminal. We both cried. I waved bye and she waved back. Later that day I got a call from Okenna that she was home with them and would be dropped off the next morning. That was the beginning of Udumaga's independent living.

She registered and began classes. Her full scholarship kicked in. But the university gave her till the end of the semester to show proof of her citizenship because the scholarship was only for citizens.

I dropped everything and began the process of applying for her citizenship. Within four weeks, she was invited for the citizenship interview. Within the next two weeks, she was sworn in. The scholarship was saved.

But after one year in Pharmacy, she called me and said, "Mom, Pharmacy is not my calling. I am doing well in it. But, it does not fulfil me". I said, tell me what your calling is. Deep inside, I knew. This girl loves to talk and argue. "My calling is Law", she told me. She changed her program to Pre-Law-Psychology. She began this new program with Financial Aid. Upon graduation she decided to reside in Houston. Her Law school was on pause. I was on her back and I prayed. I knew her strength.

She fell in love, got married. I was still on her back to pursue her calling. Years past, I was still on her back. COVID-19 global pandemic hit, she applied and was accepted to many schools in the South, East and West. She accepted one in Houston.

Prior to getting into Law school, she was a frequent writer on Facebook, making arguments on many issues that some of her friends thought she was an Attorney. I nicknamed her "Facebook Lawyer". I told her I would not react or comment on her Facebook page until she has those letters, Juris Doctor behind her name.

She finished first year with flying colors and made her Law School's Law Review. She is so passionate about Law. Her dream is to become a Judge. Already her siblings and myself call her "Judge" Emily Mitchell.

20

LEAVING ON A PRIVATE JET

A decorated and storied high school and college football wide receiver, Gilbert Onyekachi my first son, is a natural people person, with a gift of paying attention and mirroring the energy of the other person. Born in Nigeria while I was finishing my tertiary education, we lived in a Boys' Quarters, BQ as they call it in Nigeria, in the defunct Shell Camp, in Owerri.

He came to the USA as a toddler. In elementary school, he excelled and was the teacher's favorite.

I call him Onyi. His first name comes from a Mathematician who came up with Gilbert's theory. His father being a Mathematician gave him that name. I gave him Onyekachi meaning "nobody is greater than God."

He loves sports. He started playing Little League Football and proceeded to High school. In High school, he was fun to watch. He played wide receiver. He made the local Newspaper and TV stations every Friday. He also held down jobs at Chicken kitchens and Shoe stores in High School. He became a local "star" among his peers.

College Football recruits called me from around the country. They knocked on my doors, visited my office. All of the football recruits promised me that they would take good care of my son. "We throw balls, and we know he can receive the ball. He is a big receiver with great hands", all of them said to me. It was all football, football. We play the "spread passing offense". I looked blank at them. What does that mean? I asked myself. They knew I had no idea. So the explanation of what a "spread passing offense" began. We throw balls. Majority of the universities that recruited him played the spread passing offense. I travelled with him for many school visits. They lavishly treated us, parents to sumptuous dinner. They lodged us in luxury hotels. They laid the red carpet.

One university in Louisiana with a great spread passing offense informed me that they want my son to visit the school. I said sure. They said they would send a private plane to pick him up by the Lake Front Airport in New Orleans. I was reluctant. I thought about all that could go wrong. What if they crash? How would I explain that I let my beloved son fly in that small private plane? Let it not rain, I prayed.

On the other hand, I was a proud and happy mother. My son is really needed in this football team. It is a thing of joy to be needed. Who sends a private plane to pick a very young man up. That day I came. I brought him to the Lake Front Airport. The Pilot confirmed his identity, he boarded, and the plane took off. I turned my back and cried. An hour or so later, he called to inform me that they landed. He spent a night there. He was treated like a star he told me. "They play the spread passing offense and I am a wide receiver", he told me. The next day, same plane and same pilot flew him back. I picked him up. I thanked God he came back.

He kept saying, "mom, let me go to one of these spread passing offense programs". I was like, son, remember, educational excellence.

I was not buying this football thing. They told me about free tuition, room and board the next level. and they would assist him get to the next level.

I was still not buying it. After one visit to one university in the South, and seeing many of the young men, I told myself, this is not what I want for my son. Educational Excellence kept creeping into my mind, "do not forget your standard", that voice reminded me.

One day one university that plays the "triple option" called. They wanted Onyi. A highly selective university. "Harvard of the South". I jumped for joy. This is what I want, educational excellence. The football recruits hunted me down. They visited my home, my office. They shared their university's emphasis on educational excellence, raising young men. I called my family and friends and shared with them this university that wants Onyi to come play football, get his bachelor's all paid for. Everyone agreed to send him there.

The other spread passing offense recruiters were still calling and visiting. When I told them that he was going to this university, they took their time to explain to me that I should not send a highly decorated high school wide receiver to a triple option university. I thanked them. He attended the triple option university, played football, left his footprints there, received his undergraduate degree for free there. This university not only gave him a full ride, they made him a great gentleman he has become.

Onyekachi's university was the first college to "be back in the sky" right after 9/11. It was another Jet trip. It was scary but life must go on and God is always in control. Here is the link: https://www.youtube.com/watch?v=-5lgcfhogj4. Onyekachi's first appearance in the video is at 58 seconds into the video. He was featured again in the video. I was shocked that day when it was aired on ESPN.

While he was in college, he was on Federal Financial Aid. Each semester, he would hand over his refund to me. He would say, "mom, take this, you need it". A sweet son. He did not need it. They provided all that he needed. Years later on Facebook, he wrote this on his page: "…if your eyes don't tear up when you hear "Dear Mama", you probably don't have a good relationship with yours or haven't been through much with her. You couldn't tell me I wasn't the man when I was sending Pell grant money home back in the day". My response to that post was, you sure did.

Today, he is a husband, father of two, a real estate entrepreneur and still flies in a private plane for his professional job. Mama does not like that.

21

MAKE SENSE

My first "anchor" baby, Irene Obianuju was born in the USA a year after we relocated to the USA. We thought that after we have acquired "the golden fleece" we would return to Nigeria. That was not to happen. Irene became the doll of the home. Growing up, she was pampered by all. A picky eater, she loved her comfort Food-Roast beef sandwich.

Her siblings called her "drama queen". She would come back from school and tell everything that happened, demonstrating it. She loved to take care of sick ones at a very young age. She would ask: "what's wrong? Do you need medicine? I get it for you".

As early as 9th Grade, she volunteered at Tulane Hospital, Downtown, New Orleans. Every morning during summer, she dressed up in her uniform, caught City Bus and was there to help. She told us she worked as a greeter, giving visitors directions to wherever part of the hospital they were heading to. She brought ice, water to patients' rooms and followed Nurses around and assisted them with whatever they asked her to do. One day she came home and announced to me:

"Mom, I want to be a nurse". I responded, I sensed that. "I like the way nurses run to patients call for one thing or the other and help nurture the sick to get better", make sense?" Irene continued. Nursing was her calling.

But first, she returned to her hobby, speaking. She would engage in competition around town like "The Dr. Martin Luther King Jr. Essay contest". She took first place in one year's city wide contest and received a cash award. Her opening line in the essay was "To me, this essay is not about writing a 500-word essay. It's about making a difference, an impact!". Irene always makes a difference and an impact anywhere she finds herself and among individuals or groups. Irene continued her speaking engagements with her professional organizations and her businesses and other platforms such as Instagram where she established "Monday with Mother". I was her first guest on this show. Family and friends gathered to listen to me give them tips on how I raised my children to become successful. I almost botched the show. It was my first time on Instagram Live. Irene kept teaching me how to position my phone so the audience could see me well. After a few instructions, I got it, and the show continued and ended very well. That was pre pandemic COVID-19.

Irene finished High school and went off to college in the state to begin her nursing education. When she was in 12th Grade, a statewide scholarship program became available for all students who meet the criteria to attend college in the state. I told her, God has buttered our bread. You must attend college here. You will not follow your two older siblings to Houston, Texas even though you are eligible for

Texas scholarship since you were born there. She listened and understood.

The Taylor Opportunity Program for Students (TOPS); "TOPS is the Tuition Opportunity Program for Students that provides Louisiana high school graduates meeting specific eligibility requirements with a scholarship if they choose to attend a Louisiana public college or university". You can use TOPS to complete your undergraduate degree if you maintain the "specific eligibility requirements". And this, Irene did for her Bachelor's degree in Nursing. She was in Nursing School Downtown New Orleans when Hurricane Katrina hit. Hurricane Katrina was the worst natural disaster to hit New Orleans in 2005. Irene was airlifted from her dormitory rooftop to Baton Rouge where all of us were reunited.

22

YOU HEARD ME

Linda Obinwanne is the last daughter. From childhood she would cry for any little thing. The death of her father devastated her the most. She had a little idea of her Dad, always running to him as soon as he came home from work. Dad would carry her and gave her goodies. Like her middle name, Obinwanne, meaning love for siblings, she cares for all, she does not consider anyone a stranger.

Linda has a heart of gold, a very spiritual young woman. She is the "Prayer Warrior" of the family. Whatever problem, obstacle or issue any one of us has or had, you must call Linda to send it back to the "pit of hell" like she likes to say, where the problem belongs and sends you to the "King's Palace". Yes, she has prayed us to the "King's Palace".

Linda with a Master's degree in Social Work, has very strong technical skills. She can tinker with computers. Growing up, she would fix our broken computer, taught many of us, Computer skills. She wanted to pursue Computer Systems. Mama put a brake on that. But Mama did not take away those skills.

She prays during family gatherings and holidays. Her prayers are usually very long. The dinner would be cold as some family members would begin eating secretly. After so many long prayers over meals, her siblings now offer to lead in family prayers. Linda laughs when they do this. She goes along with their prayers. But she still finds a way to "preach" the Word. "Thus says the Lord, you heard me" in her unique New Orleans accent. She loves to call those of us born and raised in Africa, Africans in a loving way. We joke about this. We call her "American".

She loves to crack jokes with "Africans" as she tries to "Americanize" them.

"I am the Proverbs 31, verse 10-31 (Kings James Version) woman; she always says. "You heard me", as she preaches The Word. Often, she would type and print her sermons for all to read. It is good to have a prayer warrior, a true believer in the true meaning of the word who loves the Lord and prays for all, strangers alike.

23

I AM JUST A PEASANT

A man of few words Mike was hardly a toddler when their dad passed on. As a baby, he travelled with me to Aro Chukwu in Abia State to bury his dad. He did not know him. He would cry and rush screaming "daddy" whenever a car pulled in our drive way at Aro Chukwu. The burial was done and the funeral rites completed all bundled up because of our limited stay. Towards the end of our stay, Michael caught malaria. The trip was caught short and we flew back to the USA. He was admitted at Tulane Hospital, New Orleans in quarantine. This ordeal is narrated in Chapter 8, Malaria Parasite.

Mike was into football like his older brother, Gilbert. On finishing Elementary and Middle school, he followed his older siblings to a magnet high school in the city. He excelled, but football became his love. He played wide receiver too. A hand injury in junior and senior years kept him in the inactive injured list when scouts came at games. He applied to the state's flagship university, was accepted. I paid his deposit for room and board. A week before he would move into the dormitory, I heard a knock on my door. There were two men standing outside. They introduced themselves as Football Recruiters from a state university. I let them in. They wanted Michael. A shift began. I lost my deposit at the flagship university and drove Michael to Nicholls State University, Thibodaux (The Colonels).

As a Colonel, the fans nicknamed him "MO". MO was great on the field. He played wide receiver. We attended all his home games. MO was a big star there. MO finished college.

He tried his hands in a variety of endeavors including arena football, NFL and substitute teaching. Substitute teaching almost consumed him until one early morning.

One early morning, I woke up and went straight to Mike's room. He was getting ready to go teach. After we exchanged pleasantries, I told him to call the Principal of the school he was about to go teach, and tell him or her, that he would no longer be available. He looked at me in shock. I stood firm and said yes, today is your last day. Let us try something else. You are smart and you can do better than this. In my mind, I was hoping and praying he accepts. He was ready. The shift began to take hold. "Ogugua", I called hum. Michael began his premedical program and succeeded with flying colors. He had three medical school acceptance. One of them was for an MD/JD. We chose for him to be at a hometown school. Four years, it was over. Residency was here too. Doors were opened for him by strangers, God bless them.

A man of few words, a peasant, became a man of medicine and community service advocate. He is truly a peasant turned physician. When asked by a young lady what he was doing now, Mike responded, "I am just a peasant to the laughter of all who were present, including the young lady. No one knew his potential except himself and his Mama. Mama knows each of her children's capabilities. Mama cried on his graduation day from Medical School. Tears rolled down his Mama's eyes when his name was called out "Dr. Michael Chikwendu Okoronkwo". That day made me know that whatever has been written for one cannot be changed. Mama screamed it out in Igbo, O dera, O desigo". My friend who sat next to me at graduation witnessed my cry of joy and the journey that has brought us here. The story of the journey was not easy, but he faced it and today he looks towards the future with hope and gladness.

24

I GOT IN, I GOT IN

Nine years after I had my sixth child, I had a baby boy. It was not an easy delivery, but as would God have it, I had an excellent OBG/YN who was at my bedside until he felt it was time to operate on me. My blood pressure was hitting the roof. The doctor would intermittently ask me to identify colors. I passed the color test. He would then say let us wait a minute for the dilation to move on. I was stuck at 7.5. Finally, I had the baby. He weighed over ten pounds and very long. I had Preeclampsia. The doctor and nurses loved him. The doctor said with these long hands, he would play basketball. He played high school basketball and football. He was the quarterback for his high school football team. One day at his basketball game, Ike's team was losing. The cheerleaders started chanting: "Number 3 is going to Harvard, and no one on your team going to Harvard".

Ike as all of us lovingly called him, became the center of the family. His older siblings worked at Fast Foods (Chicken). They would bring back chicken, Ike loved the chicken. His first word was chicken which he pronounced "Kankan". Ike began his elementary school with an inquisitive mind. One day, Irene was discussing Photosynthesis with a classmate, and Ike asked, "What is Photosynthesis?" Irene responded, "child, learn how to read and write first. But, she explained to him in simple language, what it meant. Ike began early to read books above his age group, whether he understood them or not I cannot tell you.

He would inquire from his siblings about the number 1 university in the U.S.A. They told him Harvard. He said at age five, that is where I would go. In elementary school, he would cry if he had less than an "A" in an exam.

Every day, I dropped him off to school and picked him. I would bring him to my office after buying him snacks or hamburger. He would do his homework in my office or took it to the Library to sit there and complete. After he completed his homework, I began teaching him Igbo and reading Psalm 23 in Igbo. I had an Igbo Bible in my office that stayed opened to Psalm 23. Psalm 23 kept me anchored around the chaos. Ike enjoyed reading Psalm 23. Then, he was eight years old.

The Igbo organization of New Orleans began planning an Igbo Day celebration. I was excited. It took me back to my Igbo Union Day celebration in Kaduna. Our Igbo children in New Orleans were encouraged to engage in activities such as dance, song etc. I volunteered Ike to recite Psalm 23 in Igbo. Mothers were worried that we did not have time for him to learn and recite this. I assured them that he would not embarrass us. They accepted. Ike went for practice for other activities and for his recitation. One of the grandmothers who was visiting her daughter helped sharpen his recitation skills. The day came. The young boys and girls were dressed in our cultural attires. The girls displayed their dance skills taught to them by two young mothers. It was Ike's turn to recite Psalm 23 in Igbo. He was called to the stage. I held my breath. He took the microphone. To the amazement of all, he did not stammer not stumble. He recited it to a standing ovation. My people sprayed him. One can find this in YouTube: <u>IGBO DAY Celebration, by NDIGBO DEVELOPMENT ORG., New Orleans 2005 - YouTube</u>. This event took place a week before Hurricane Katrina, the worst hurricane to have hit New Orleans, Louisiana.

Ike's journey continued in North Louisiana where we relocated and lived with his Dad. He enrolled in a university elementary school. My job transferred to this university temporarily until we moved back to New Orleans. In this school he tells me, a teacher always made them recite this: "I am the Best, It is not because I am better than the others, it is because I sit among the Best".

He was focused on going to Harvard early. He focused. He applied for Early Admit. In early December of the year he applied, I was in my office when my phone rang. It was Ike. He screamed, "I got in, I got in". I too screamed. I advised him to drive home safely and I would meet him there. He had scholarships, McDonald, Allstate Sugar Bowl. He was featured on Television and Newspapers for going to Harvard and winning scholarships. Harvard was the only university he applied to, though many universities offered him full ride.

He graduated from Harvard to another Ivy League, Brown for Medical School. Today, he is finishing his intern year in Orthopedic Medicine.

25

IGBO UNION

Then, in Kaduna, Igbo Union Day was huge in Kaduna, in fact outside Igbo land in Nigeria. But I remember Kaduna because I was born in that city and began my primary school education there. During Igbo Day Celebration, it was always festive. Our mothers would gather all the girls three months before the event to teach us our language, culture and dance for presentation on that event day. They taught us the ways of our ancestors. They did not fail us. Our fathers did the same with our brothers. All Igbo children looked forward to it. We looked forward to Bata shoes, new clothes, rice and stew "very plenty".

My father was a very strong Igbo man, who loved his language and culture. One of his happiest days was Igbo Union Day when he would display his artistic and acrobatic Aro Chukwu dance moves. He loved to sing Ojojo songs. He spoke pure Aro dialect without mincing words. He spoke in idioms and Proverbs literally and figuratively. He would tell us for example: aka mere n'ite, ite jiri mee kponkorum", meaning, literally, if you behave yourself,

I would not be talking too much. He loved us all, and believed we could get to the sky and beyond. He always had "a feeling". We affectionately called him, "I have a feeling". A hard working man who provided for his family. On Igbo Union Day, he proudly took his three sons, my brothers with him. When I was ready for secondary school later after the war, I remember hearing my father telling a cousin of his, that he would manage to send me to secondary school regardless of the cost. At this time, my two older siblings were in secondary schools and this cousin was of the opinion that my father could not afford to have three children in secondary schools at the same time. My father's response to him was: "there is no harm in trying".

My father died in my arms. That was when I had my first baby at Enugu. After three months, I brought her to Nzerem to prepare for "Nkuputa Nwa m", meaning baby outing. I came to buy the best original and authentic Igbo foodstuff. I was to spend two weeks. One early morning, I was still in bed with my baby and my mother was busy with chores when we heard commotion coming from the only main road in the town. We ran out to see what was going on. A voice screamed: "Miss, your dad has been hit by a drunk driver". I handed my baby to an aunty, ran with my mother as fast as we could. A bus was on fire. The youth set it on fire. The driver escaped. If he had not escaped, it could have been Jungle Justice for him. We rushed my father in a bus to the closet hospital which was twenty miles away. In the bus was one of my distant aunties. She asked the driver to wait a minute; she came back with her handbag. At the hospital, the doctor tried to resuscitate my father. It was too late. The doctor declared him dead. There was wailing. I was worried for my mother as I held her. The distant auntie opened her handbag and pulled out the "omu Aro" wrapper and covered my father. This was significant I was later told. An Aro man or woman must be covered in "omu Aro". In addition to omu Aro, he wore his "Isi Agu" regalia to lie in state. The Isi Agu was my gift to him when I received my arrears after passing all my papers in one sitting. My father said to me: whenever I die, I bury me in this". "I have a feeling", always had his feelings come true. He was a true Igbo/Aro man.

Our mothers introduced us to the traditional call and response of Igbo story telling. "O-t-i", they would call, and we responded "oyo". This had to be repeated three times. They told us stories about the tortoise and its cunning behavior. Then, they began teaching us songs along with their dance steps. Our mothers were truly our role models.

One of my favorite songs was: Umu aka Igbo, anyi a biala (three times)

Umu aka Igbo, ndi anyi ji e mee ngagala, anyi biala. Na ngwanu, n'ike unu, were nu ya gawa. (Our Igbo children, are here, the children who make us proud, go ahead with your show). The other song our mothers taught us was: "Onye ihe m n'ewe ewe, Ya biko wegbu ya, chorus is Ndasariwa", Oyoyo nwanne, ya biko wegbu ya., Ya biko wegbue ya, Ndansariwa" (If you are mad with me, get madder).

We sang and we practiced. We had dancers, instrument players (ogene, ekwe, udu), and singers. I was one of the dancers and singers. Like mother like daughter, a saying goes. My mother was a singer and dancer for the Igbo Union, Kaduna branch.

On the celebration day, our mothers dressed us up with wrappers on the bottom and one smaller wrapper on our chest. As we performed, we were sprayed graciously and richly.

At the end of every event, we changed clothes to our new clothes and Bata shoes. Igbo Union had a song for Bata shoes which goes like this: Mgbe anyi na-eme inyanga (twice), akpukpu ukwu anyi na-ada n'koolta, kpoi, kpoi". When we strut on the street, our shoes went, click, click. There were many takeaways from my Igbo Union experience. They include taking pride in my culture, in my identity and my language. I shall never forget.

26

AZU OZE

Before the Nigeria Civil war began, we relocated from Mbala to Nzerem. In Nzerem, we resided with my paternal family. We remained there for about seven months before the place was threatened by the fast approaching war. My mother decided to take us, my two older sisters, my younger brothers and myself to a safer city. My father decided to stay "behind" with my older brother. We walked for more than twenty hours before we arrived at a safe city. We were placed in a school hall, called "Refugee Hall", We had a "corner" with all our stuff. There were more than fifty families housed there. There was a soup kitchen.

After a short stay in this city, the city began to "fall" to Enemy territory. Another very long walk across creeks, rivers and bridges. Mothers carried their belongings on their heads and had their babies on their backs. In this long walk, we walked with friendly soldiers who would destroy bridges as everyone crossed the bridges. We walked from this city, Ugwueke to Ohafia in Abia state. It took hours. At Ohafia, a lorry picked us up for Aro Chukwu. That was when I turned ten years old.

At Aro Chukwu, my hometown, we settled down, my mother, one of my sisters and me. My other sister and brothers were picked up by my aunties at Ugwueke. We lived.

I started school at my village school to finish my elementary school. One morning, my mother told me to dress up, she was going to enroll me in school. We walked about two miles on the gravel and dusty road. She took me to the headmaster's office and registered me. Off, I went to my Elementary six class. The teacher taught us Mathematics and English, History, Geography etc. She taught us how to write winning essays. We were taught to memorize the multiplication table, big spelling words, capitals of countries along with each country's President. Most of us were brilliant. The teacher was preparing us for the First School Leaving Certificate. After school, some of us stayed behind to quiz ourselves, tutor ourselves in Mathematics, spelling and the meaning of those big words. Truth be told, some of us, not just me, were seriously preparing for this examination. Passing the examination very well was our gateway to select secondary schools. We sat for the First School Leaving Certificate, the result was never released before the war ended. At school, we were fed "Charistas" meals. Bombs disrupted our living and learning. I learnt much in that school, from enhancing my grasp of the English language to learning much about the world. The western world was taught to us, especially, The U.S.A. I remember our teacher teaching us about this place, a place of opportunity, an American wonderland. Many of us dreamt of America. We dreamt of reaching this promise land. A few of us reside in this place.

Aro Chukwu is remotely located far away from main towns where the battlegrounds were. One fine day, a fighter plane was dropping bombs at Aro Chukwu. We were running in opposite direction from the plane. We could see blood and bodies. After the fighter plane stopped, it was announced that all is encouraged to move into Azu Oze. I wondered, and remained deeply in shock. Azu Oze, I kept reflecting. We entered the forest with the much we could take with us. Mothers balanced belongings on their heads. In the forest, yams were roasted at night to avoid attracting fighter planes.

Azu Oze was a marshy forest in one end of the village. There was a stream at this forest. There was no house, except for the tree shades. Then, in this forest, you could not see the sky. This was our abode with other families for two weeks until it was announced that the war has ended.

27

MAMA PRODUCTION COMPANY

I was born a year after the Queen of England visited Nigeria for the first time. I was born Mgboro Reuben Ezuma Igwe at Kaduna, named after my maternal grandma. "I looked like her", they said. I am the fifth of seven children, the last girl of four girls. I am between my three brothers; I am right behind our oldest brother, and the other two brothers came after me. My father worked for the Railway Station and my mother was a petty trader of fruits and snacks. I was not spoilt. My mother would often tell us to "manage; manage this, manage that". I have since growing up heard some women say, that all their lives they never "managed", that their parents never told them to "manage". Even in my elementary school in Kaduna, I was taught a song that some of the lyrics I remember go like this: I am content with what I have". This early lesson of management and contentment laid the foundation of my strength to survive in my early obstacles. My children often joke with me and say, "manage it". Whenever I shared with them the little money I had,

I would tell them "manage it", apply "opportunity cost". Then, they were still young. They would ask me' "what is opportunity cost?". In secondary school, I took Economics using a book by a famous Nigerian author of Economics, Lawal. So I would recall my secondary school days' lesson in "opportunity cost". Sometimes, when I cooked for the week, I would warn them that this is for the week, if you finish it before then, I will look at you and you will look at me". We survived, we did not miss a meal, but we managed. My mama often reminded me not to spoil my children, to raise them instead of raising your house help. I did not have house help. My mother also spoke with idioms and proverbs. She would say, "si n'ala ririe, gbago n'table", karia, I si na table ririe kpadata n'ala" - meaning it is better to start from the ground and move up, instead of starting from the top and going down" While growing up in Nigeria, I observed that many families worked their house helps sixteen hours a day while their children lived a luxurious lifestyle. Many of these children do not know how to clean, sweep and do household chores. They are spoilt. Later in life, many of the house helps become self-sufficient, completing college whereas the "big men's children often fall on the way side, become dependent on parents until their parents pass away. Then they sit on Daddy's wealth and squander it in months. To be sure, not all "big men's" children are spoilt.

I was exposed to diversity and inclusion early in life. I started my elementary education at a school in Kaduna, where every "tribe and tongue" was represented. We interacted with one another, played together during recess, ate together and studied together. Language was never a barrier to us. If one of us could not understand the other's ethnic language like Hausa, Igbo or Yoruba, we resorted to the language we all spoke, English, be it "Broken English".

Every morning in class, we recited our Multiplication Table and did "Mental" Test in Mathematics. For the mental test, we must not use paper and pencil, every question must be done "mentally", you must add, subtract, multiply and divide, use "BODMAS" in your head. It was fun if you successfully answered your questions. But if you failed any, you received a "ruler". The teacher used his or her ruler to flog you. If you failed one question, you got one ruler, but if you failed four you received four rulers and so on and so forth. One student failed all six mental test one morning. The teacher was mad.

"Come in front of the class and receive your six flogs", the teacher said to John. Usually the teacher would walk up to the student to flog. But this morning was different.

John looked around and said, "Sir, are you referring to me?"

The teacher got furious. "If you open your mouth and ask me one more question, I will double the flogs. You must do your homework, prepare to come to school. A farmer does not forget his or her cutlass at home before going to the farm. Come here now, John", the teacher exclaimed.

John walked up to the front. The teacher approached him with his ruler. "Open your hand", the teacher said. John complied. The teacher announced to the class, to begin counting after each flog. The first flog, the class shouted in unison, "one". The second flog came, we shouted, "two". As the teacher raised his hand for the third flog, John dashed for the door and fled. That was the last we saw John. We heard he transferred to another school. The teacher did not stop the morning Mental Test and the flogging.

Linda, my last daughter nicknamed me "Production Company". According to her, none of her siblings fell on the way side. I produced, she said. Each one is accomplished in his or her own right. I often challenged them to go out there and compete, dominate. Your peers and others who are making it do not have "two heads". My parents told me that as well as my grandmother, uncles and aunties. Production company fell back to her own upbringing beginning at home, going through secondary school and beyond. My secondary school experience was highly structured, time to wake up, time to clean, time to pray, time for breakfast, time for classes, time for lunch, then nap time. From the moment you wake up to the time you close your eyes to sleep at night, it was structured and timed.

In my class one in the select secondary school, I must have displayed some early element of special talent, of intelligence. The teachers seemed to favor me. I would always raise my hand to answer questions. Almost all the time, my answers were right. There were two other girls in my class who competed with me. Three of us became close friends; we studied together and excelled. We were in Class 1A, that meant we must represent very well to belong to class A. Then, a student was placed in Class A, B, C, or D depending on your academic ranking. Class A students represented those who scored all "As", or close to that. Class B, meant "b" average students and so on and so forth. So, to maintain Class A status, a student in such a class would work hard to maintain it. Such a student would want to be promoted to the next class of A, for example Class 2A. My two classmates and I always flipped 1ˢᵗ, 2ⁿᵈ and 3ʳᵈ positions at the end of each term. It was hard work.

I transferred to another school at Abakaliki. It was a mixed school for boys and girls. I continued to excel. I became a student female leader-senior Prefect for Girls. As a student leader I gave announcements. I would take my time to seriously prepare for my announcement. This was a time a student leader must display his or her knowledge of the English language. Your intonation and command of the language must be perfect. If you made a mistake, for example and used the wrong verb, you would be nicknamed. I graduated in flying colors and went into teaching.

Then, Nigeria was great. The government paid for my Crash Teacher Training. All one had to be concerned with was one's transportation money to and fro. In my three-year Advanced Teacher Training at Alvan Ikoku College of Education, Owerri, the same was the case. I had a free ride. The federal government paid for tuition, housing and meals. Again, students only were concerned for their transportation. I lived in well-kept housing, had free balanced meals along with special meals on Sundays. Every student who travelled for the weekend always came back early to partake in the special Sunday Lunch. Well air conditioned luxurious buses plied the roads. These buses played soft music that relaxed one. There was no fear of armed robbery, or kidnapping. Nigeria was good then. We had financial book support from the federal government to cover our book supplies. Then, Nigeria was good. Professors were returning home from abroad including the U.S.A. I had a few of my lecturers who just returned from the U.S.A. Some of them shared stories in class about their experiences. My areas of concentration were English/Igbo. That was in the 1980s.

My English classes were on the second floor of the Language Building. Across from this building, there was the Science Building. Dr. Chima was one of my English Literature lecturers. He was just the best. One day as he was teaching, he looked through the window and saw a car pulling up. He stopped teaching and called our attention to the car. "That's my wife, he said, I met her in America. She is Igbo and beautiful and smart too. She teaches Chemistry, she taught me the chemistry of love". The entire class burst into cheers and applause. They met in the university they both attended. They earned their terminal degrees in their respective fields of concentration.

A female professor of Education, a very petite woman, London trained, would not teach a class if a male student had a cap on in class. She would lecture about gentleman's behavior. Some of these young male students would hesitate removing their caps and the professor would pick her handbag and books to leave, the entire class would shout at those young men to remove their caps or leave. They obliged. Professor Nkemji was a very smart woman with strong vocabulary. When she taught, same young men with caps would say, "Prof, can you repeat yourself, the smart lecturer would say, "I have so many verbs in my pockets, I cannot remember what I just said" to the laughter of the class. Professor Nkemji would tell us stories about London, how you must be independent, and how nobody would hold your hand to show you where the tap is. You all better be serious with yourselves, she admonished us.

28

CHEAT CHAPTER

It is really hard for me to provide a cheat sheet. I only use a cheat sheet when I present. In my presentations, I write, rewrite my presentation. As I am writing and rewriting, I am reading it without making effort to memorize it for a well-rehearsed speech. It is just automatic that as I write and rewrite, read and read over it several times, it gets stuck in my head. In case, I forget something, my cheat sheet comes in handy. I did not have a written cheat sheet that I used when I was raising my children. I relied on how I was raised by my parents, grandmother, aunties and uncles and other village men and women who played a role in raising me. Where I come from, it takes the entire village, not just your immediate parents to raise one. That was my cheat sheet. In this place (USA), you are kind of on your own, unless you are linked to a few great families and community associations, then, they can sort of serve as your village.

My cheat sheet begins with making God the central pillar of your home. You have to start early, when they are still very young as young as one-year-old. Take them with you to worship. Pray in your household. Be consistent and persistent.

In whatever you do and want to do with your child/children, do not be "shaky, shaky, Alawo". Be consistent.

Does gene pool matter? Let me put out a disclaimer right away, I am not a Scientist. But I think, that gene pool matters. But the right environment super matters. You may have all the gene pool, mother might be super smart, and dad too, but you cannot let your resources raise them. Resource alone does not raise children. You must be present in their lives. You must follow them, not just worrying about how many followers you have on Instant Gram, Facebook and the other social media handles. Follow your children to see what they are doing, who they are hanging out with. Know your children's friends and their parents. If any of their friends do not appear to have goals, gently explain to your children to evaluate their friends, if their goals do not match their own, run "four forty" like I told my children.

Another strong pillar you need is an educational excellence pillar. Let your children understand and appreciate that education is a great "equalizer". Let your children know that other successful children in your community, do not have "two heads". If those ones can do it, you too can do it. Whether you are from a poor home or rich home, single home or two parent home, education is a huge equalizer for one to sit at a table with kings, queens, headhunters and others. It must start early, not in the 9th Grade. It starts in kindergarten. It is not an easy task; it is a very daunting task. Some of the children will understand it early and embrace it, while others can be "late bloomers". That's okay too. You just have to know that "a mother gives birth to all her children, but each child's chi is different", an Igbo proverb states. This proverb validates individual differences. Allow each child to become what his or her chi has set him or her to become.

Have a vision for your children; let each child create his or her own vision. But whatever the vision, do not tie it to someone else's resources.

You have to be judicious in your relationships. You have to treat everyone without fail, with dignity and respect. Some people want to be popular and all that, but you cannot be everything to everybody. It is not being elitist. Some people you just have a "hi, bye" relationship; and others with your type of vision, you must keep them close to you.

Do not forget to pray for your children. Call each of them by his or her name, as you lift them up.

Every body's journey is unique and different. This is my journey. It was not perfect and I am still on my journey. Our journeys do not end until we reach our expiration day, date and time.

Printed in the United States
by Baker & Taylor Publisher Services